S0-BYV-582

Your Environment

Food and the WORLD

Julia Allen & Margaret Iggulden

Stargazer Books

How to use this book

This series has been developed for group use in the classroom, as well as for students reading alone. Its text on two levels allows students of mixed reading abilities to enjoy reading and talking about the same topic.

(1) The main text and (2) picture captions give essential information in short, simple sentences. They are set in the © Sassoon font, recommended for maximum legibility. This font style helps students bridge the gap between their reading and writing skills.

(3) Below each picture caption is a subtext that explains the pictures in greater detail, using more complicated sentence structures and vocabulary.

(4) Text backgrounds are cream or a soft yellow to reduce the text/background contrast to support students with visual processing difficulties or other special needs.

Introduction

Food and water are the (1) **two most important things needed for life.**

⬆ **These children live** (2) **in India. They do not have enough food or clean water.**

Nepal, Bangladesh, and Tanzania (3) are developing countries. (4)

© Aladdin Books Ltd 2007

Designed and produced by
Aladdin Books Ltd

First published in the
United States in 2007 by
Stargazer Books
c/o The Creative Company
123 South Broad Street
P.O. Box 227
Mankato, Minnesota 56002

Printed in the United States
All rights reserved

Picture Research:
Gemma Cooper

Educational Consultant:
Jackie Holderness

Food and the World Consultant:
Clare Oxborrow

Design: Ken Vail Graphic Design,
Cambridge, UK

Library of Congress Cataloging-
in-Publication Data

Allen, Julia.
   Food and the world / by Julia Allen
   and Margaret Iggulden.
     p. cm. -- (Your environment)
   ISBN 978-1-59604-065-6
     1. Food--Juvenile literature. 2. Food supply-
-Developing countries--Juvenile literature. I.
Iggulden, Margaret. II. Title. III. Series.

TX355.A47 2005
641.3--dc22

2005042656

CONTENTS

JUN 0 4 2007

Introduction

Food and water are the two most important things needed for life. Without them no animals, including humans, or plants can survive.

There are over six billion people in the world. Every day that number grows.

It is a constant struggle to provide food and water for all the people in the world.

⬆ **Many are starving.**

There are 800 million people who don't have enough food to eat. There is not enough food available in the right place at the right time.

◁ **India is a developing country. Many people living there do not have enough food or clean water.**

Nepal, Bangladesh, and Tanzania are also developing countries. Most of the people are poor, with not enough food to eat, or clean water to drink.

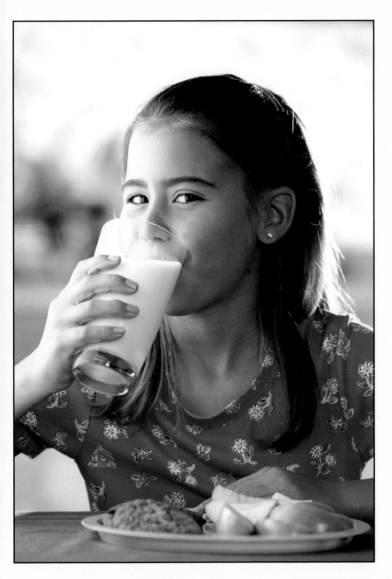

⬆ **The United States, Canada, and Britain are examples of developed countries.**

Australia, France, and Japan are some other developed countries. People here have enough food, and access to clean water. Most have homes and jobs, and children can go to school. Many families even earn enough money to go on vacations, too.

⬇ **Everyone in the world should be able to have safe, healthy food every day.**

October 16th is World Food Day. This reminds us that we can all learn more about how to help people in the world who are hungry.

In this book we find out why people are hungry and what kind of crops are grown in developing countries. We look, too, at food and farming throughout the world.

Who's fed? Who's hungry?

Every day, over one billion people try to feed themselves on less than 80 cents a day.

Millions of children die each year from hunger and related illnesses.

This need not happen. In 2000, the United Nations said that by 2015 it would halve the number of people who suffer from hunger in the world.

▷ **People in developed countries are able to buy food.**

Most people living in industrial countries earn enough money to buy plenty of food. Sadly, a lot of food is thrown away and wasted.

◁ Changes in developing countries have led to changes in people's diet.

In fast-developing countries like China, diets have changed in less than 30 years. The simple, healthy food they used to eat has been replaced by unhealthy processed food. This has created a generation of overweight children.

▽ More people now eat meat.

People eat meat all over the world, but mainly in developed countries. The amount of meat eaten is increasing. Therefore, more land is used to graze cattle. A piece of land that supports enough cattle to feed two people would feed sixty if planted with corn.

△ There are many ways to help the hungry people of the world.

Many children in developing countries do not get enough food. Some organizations like Oxfam raise money to try to help these starving people.

Maybe you can raise money for an organization to help. Get your friends together and wash cars; sell things you don't want. Try to come up with other ideas for fundraising at school.

Being healthy and living longer

What you eat is very important to your health.

Eating healthy food and exercising every day will help you live longer. There is a link between what you eat and your body's ability to fight diseases.

Too much salt and fat in your diet can damage your health. Avoid fried foods and eat more high-fiber cereals, fruits, and vegetables.

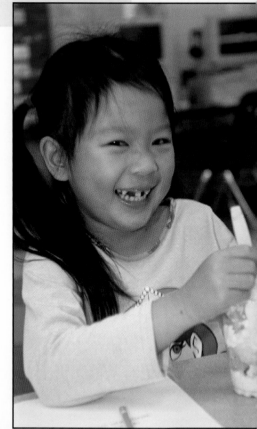

▷ **People live longer in developed countries.**

Men live to about 75 and women until 79. If you don't smoke or drink alcohol you may live even longer. In developed countries people have money to buy food, and if they are ill they can go to the doctor.

People who eat fresh fruit and vegetables are healthier.

Vegetarians are 30% less likely to get heart disease than people who eat meat. By eating a low-fat, nutritious diet, people can lower their risk of heart disease. Red meat contains protein, but it is high in fat and cholesterol. Fish and chicken are both low in fat and high in protein. In Western countries, people eat a meat-rich diet, and the level of heart disease is high. In Eastern countries, for example, Japan, fish is eaten more than meat and the level of heart disease is low.

People in developing countries die younger.

In Mozambique, a developing country, most people live to about 41. In 2005, for every 1,000 babies born there, 130 died. (In the U.S. that figure is 6 out of 1,000.) This is due to poverty and the lack of fresh food and water. In the capital, Maputo, children search trashcans for food.

A healthy diet is very important. Start your day well with a healthy breakfast.

Eat at least five portions or more of fresh fruit and vegetables every day. This helps to provide you with essential vitamins and minerals. You also need protein from fish, meat, nuts, or pulses.

Avoid eating too much salt and sugar. Remember to drink lots of water. Try to avoid too much food that is processed. Food free from chemicals is best. Look for organic fruit and vegetables.

Feeding the world

Many people in developing countries go hungry, suffering from starvation or malnutrition. If there is little rainfall, they cannot grow enough food.

In some countries, there is no work and people can't afford to buy food. In other countries, wars prevent people from farming and producing food. It is then difficult to get food to the people who need it.

◁ **There is more than enough food to go around.**

If the food produced this year were shared equally, there would be more than enough to feed everyone. However, it is not shared out properly. The developed countries account for 30% of the world. Yet they consume 60% of the world's food.

◁ Vegetables are a staple part of an African's diet.

Many farmers keep animals or hunt for meat and fish. They also grow crops, rice, corn, and millet to supplement their diet. In Zambia, Nshima, a dish made of white cornmeal, is eaten with every meal.

◁ A lot of food in developed countries is wasted.

Because there is so much choice, many people buy more than they can use. One fifth of all the food in the U.S. is thrown away. This would be enough to feed a large number of starving people.

⬇ "Live Aid" raised millions of dollars to help starving people.

In 1984, music star Bob Geldof raised awareness of the plight of starving Ethiopians. A huge concert, on two continents, was organized. The money raised has been helping these people. The event was repeated in 2005 when the Live 8 concerts raised the issue of world poverty once again.

Looking after our soil

We rely on the earth's soil to grow our crops. It is important to stop the soil eroding, or wearing away.

Clearing rain forests may give land for grazing, but it also upsets the balance of nature.

In times of heavy rains, less trees can lead to more flooding. This will result in soil erosion.

◁ **Crop rotation helps keep the soil healthy.**

Farmers have been rotating crops for hundreds of years. This means changing the types of crops grown on a piece of land on a regular basis. For example, growing clover helps to replace nitrogen that other crops need.

⬑ Once destroyed, soil cannot be replaced.

Forests and hedges provide roots that hold soil in place. As more land is cleared for farming, the soil is more vulnerable to erosion from wind and floods.

⬑ Cereal grains like wheat, corn, and rice are the most important group of crops.

Vast areas of the U.S. and Russia account for a large part of the worldwide production of wheat and corn. In other countries, smaller-scale farming is much more intensive and drains the soil of its minerals much more quickly. The soil may then become infertile.

⬑ Without soil there would be no crops.

Animals and humans rely on the soil, and the plants growing in it for survival. However, each year about 24 billion tons of soil is lost, due to bad farming, drought, or erosion. This results in less land to grow food.

Basic farming

In developing countries, many people growing food are subsistence farmers. They only produce enough to feed their families. Nothing is left over to sell to earn money.

In parts of Africa, for example, many people grow corn and some sugar cane, and keep some chickens and goats.

If these farmers could produce more of certain crops to sell as cash crops, they could then buy other things they need locally.

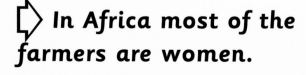 **In Africa most of the farmers are women.**

They hoe the land and sow the seeds. They tend the plants and harvest them when they are ripe. In some parts of Kenya, potatoes are grown. The women sell them by the side of the road. Others carry them in bags balanced on their heads to sell at the local market.

◁ Organizations are helping people to help themselves.

Christiana was finding it difficult to feed her family. Farm Africa loaned her a pair of goats about nine years ago, which have since had ten goats. She puts their manure onto her crops and can feed their milk to her family. The crops have grown so well she can now feed her family. She is also training other farmers.

▷ Natural methods are used in sustainable farming.

Sustainable farming is a way of growing and maintaining healthy soil, crops, and livestock on a farm. Crops are grown as naturally as possible. Manure and compost are used instead of fertilizers. The animals are fed natural foods. No pesticides are used and the food is sold as near as possible to the farm. This reduces the distance the food travels. So the food is also seasonal and fresh.

▽ Sustainable farming can help farmers in developing countries.

It is believed that sustainable farming is preferable where soil is overused and infertile. By using manure instead of expensive chemicals, farmers can fertilize the soil cheaply. With fertile soil, small farms in developing countries can grow enough food for the farmer, and extra to sell for profit.

Climate crisis

Some scientists believe pollution, including carbon dioxide from airplanes, cars, and factories, is causing global warming. This means the earth's temperatures are rising. Ice caps and glaciers are melting.

Our climate is changing, leading to more storms and floods. Too much rain destroys crops. Too little causes drought.

This will have a great impact on the world's production of food.

◁ A lack of rain leads to famine, as crops fail.

In Sudan and Ethiopia there were terrible famines in the late 20th century because rains didn't come and the crops therefore failed. Even those farmers who used to produce just enough for themselves were hit. These are poor countries, unable to buy in all the food they need to feed their people.

⬅ The number of droughts is increasing as climates change.

Crops need water to grow. Due to climate change, there have been some years when there has been no rain at all in Sub-Saharan Africa. Australia recently suffered its worst droughts for years. Farmers that lose crops and animals are unable to make a living.

⬆ Countries suffer from flooding, due to increased rainfall.

In Central America, frequent floods have destroyed crops and caused large loss of life. Many trees have been cut down, which has loosened the soil. The heavy rains turn it to mud and wash it away.

⬇ You can help stop global warming.

Although some global warming may be natural, scientists believe that we are mostly responsible. By pumping too many gases into the atmosphere, and by cutting down huge areas of forests, we have upset the natural balance.

We can all act now to help reduce pollution. Recycle as much as possible and switch those lights off! Ride a bicycle, go by bus, or walk to school instead of going by car. If this isn't possible, start a car pool. This will cut down the amount of carbon dioxide produced.

Water and irrigation

In developed countries, we take clean drinking water for granted.

But in many developing countries it is more difficult to get fresh water. Women and children often walk miles to a well or a river to fetch it.

Water is also necessary for vegetables, fruit, and other crops to grow well. In dry spells or areas, farmers may need to provide water to their crops using irrigation.

▷ **Villagers are learning about clean water.**

This woman is teaching villagers in Tanzania about the importance of keeping water clean. Dirty water may contain germs that cause disease.

Without clean drinking water we cannot live.

Contaminated water can cause the rapid spread of life-threatening diseases. Every year, between two and five million people die from drinking dirty or contaminated water. A large number of these are children who die from diarrhea, caused by drinking dirty water.

Some crops are very thirsty.

Some crops like rice and sugar cane need lots of water. However, they are grown in places like West Africa where there is little rain. If wheat, for example, were planted instead, the water would be used more efficiently.

Farmers need water for their crops.

In dry areas where there is not enough rain, farmers use various methods to water their crops. In developed countries, irrigation pipes may carry water to the crops. However, in developing countries like parts of Asia and Africa, farmers must find ways to get the most from the little rainfall there is. They cut into the hills to make terraces. Here crops are watered as rain flows down the hillside.

Food and the environment

Many farmers in developed countries use fertilizers. Pesticides are also used to poison the insects that eat the crops.

Despite a lot of testing, we still do not know what effects, if any, these chemicals have on humans. We do know they can affect wildlife. Peregrine falcon eggs became soft and weak after the adults ate animals that had fed on crops sprayed by the pesticide DDT.

⬆ Half of all fruit and vegetables sold contain amounts of some pesticides.

Farmers can now choose from about 450 pesticides. These are made from chemicals, and are designed to kill the animals that eat crops. There is still much debate about how much these pesticides affect human health.

Farmers are overusing land.

Some farmers, particularly in developing countries, are working their land too hard. There are fears that such intensive farming is destroying the delicate layer of soil. Land that is overused and never given a chance to recover will eventually become infertile. Then, little or nothing will grow.

Rachel Carson's book changed a president's mind.

While doing environmental research fifty years ago, U.S. scientist Rachel Carson found that chemicals were badly affecting the land and the animals. President John F. Kennedy read her book "Silent Spring" and banned DDT and certain other chemicals.

Thousands of acres of forest are being cut down. This is called deforestation.

Farmers in developing countries use the "slash and burn" method to clear forests. They cut the trees, burn the roots, and grow whatever they can. They sell the wood to developed countries and move on. These forests are the lungs of the world. We need trees to create the oxygen that we breathe. They also absorb the carbon dioxide that we, and much of our pollution, release into the air.

Organic vs GM food

The number of people in the world is growing and there are debates about how to *feed* them.

Some people are in favor of GM— genetically modified crops. The genes in these plants are altered to produce a crop that is, say, resistant to disease.

Others believe that we should not alter the genetic structure of our plants. They favor a return to farming naturally.

▷ **Each year more and more people are buying organic food.**

Organic food is food that is grown as naturally as possible, without the use of pesticides or fertilizers. There are very strict rules about how the crops can be grown. Animals can then graze in fields that are free of chemicals.

◁ More farmers are changing to organic farming.

They believe that organic farming is better for people's health. They also think it is better for wildlife and the environment. Organically produced meat doesn't contain antibiotics or artificial growth hormones.

⬆ This farmer practices organic methods.

The farmer of this land ensures that his crops are grown organically. No fertilizers are used to supplement the crops being grown and no pesticides are used. The crops are rotated regularly to ensure that the best use is made of the soil. Cattle that graze the land are either used for milk production or reared for beef. Both the milk and beef is sold locally.

⬇ GM crops can be designed to grow more food.

The world population is increasing rapidly and more food will be required. Supporters of GM say that their crops will produce better yields than organic crops. They will

also be resistant to pests. It is argued that GM crops like corn and soy have been grown for years without causing problems. Those opposed to GM say it is too soon to know whether health hazards exist.

Fair Trade

Fair Trade is an organization set up to promote and sell products of developing countries.

It was started to help poor farmers get a fair price for their crops. At the same time, they have to ensure that their goods are of a high quality and they have to look after the environment.

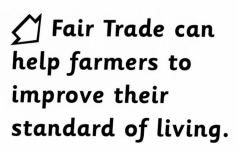 Fair Trade can help farmers to improve their standard of living.

Selling food at agreed prices can help families in developing countries climb out of poverty. They can earn money from their crops to buy other foods and goods. Workers also have rights and are less likely to be exploited.

⬅ Coffee and cocoa are two crops that are famous for the "Fair Trade" label.

Most coffee farmers in Haiti work small farms. Now, by working together as a cooperative organized by a big coffee company, they all share their animals and machinery. They are more efficient and are paid more for their produce.

⬅ Trade practices can leave farmers at risk.

Developed and developing countries have traded together for many years. For example, Caribbean farmers have sold their bananas to developed countries, such as the U.S. and Europe. However, some developed countries are now buying bananas from other, cheaper, sources. If they buy them from, say, Ecuador instead, they may seriously endanger the livelihood of the Caribbean farmers. The Fair Trade organization at least begins to protect groups of farmers in developing countries.

⬇ We can help people out of poverty by buying Fair Trade goods.

There are lots of Fair Trade products you can buy in stores now—toasted coconut, dried pineapple, and chocolate. There's Fair Trade tea and coffee, as well as fresh fruit.

Food companies generally believe that their customers want to buy good quality products at the lowest price. But more and more people now think that this is unfair to the developing countries and support the idea of Fair Trade.

25

Transporting food

In the last thirty years the kinds of food available in developed countries has changed. There is far more variety and it comes from all over the world.

A lot of our food is shipped or flown in from faraway countries. It is taken by road or railroad to distribution depots. It is then delivered by truck to stores.

▷ **Fruit and vegetables are being transported from country to country.**

Much of the food in our stores has traveled thousands of miles. Some foods are imported because they won't grow in our climate. For example, bananas come from countries such as Costa Rica and Ecuador. Others are imported because we want food that is out of season at home. When out of season, apples may come from Chile or New Zealand.

⬆ Live animals are also transported long distances.

Each year, millions of live animals—cattle, sheep, pigs, and horses—are transported across Europe. These journeys can last from 30 to 90 hours. The European Union has now stated that drivers must stop every eight hours to rest, feed, and water the animals.

◁ Transporting food all over the world means that the environment suffers.

Moving food by road, rail, or ship adds to traffic pollution. Eating locally grown produce would help reduce this pollution of the environment and helps local farmers. We would also protect local varieties, of apples, say.

⬇ Animal welfare organizations believe animals should be slaughtered near the farm.

This would ensure that animals did not have to travel far. In Australia, live animals are taken on ships to the Middle East. This puts a lot of pressure on the animals. Slaughtering animals before they are transported also reduces the risk of disease spreading.

Food and health risks

Lots of people worry about the health aspects of our food. They are concerned about the chemicals in our food, as well as the use of GM crops.

Scares about food hygiene and animal diseases highlight the need to carefully monitor food hygiene.

▷ **Shellfish should be eaten with care.**

Shrimp, mussels, and other shellfish are popular foods that are safe to eat. But they should be fresh and from clean water. Dirty seas can produce mussels that are full of pollution and dangerous to eat. Frozen shellfish and other seafood must always be defrosted carefully before cooking.

⬆ **Cows were slaughtered because of "mad cow disease."**

In the 1990s, a number of people died in the UK from eating contaminated beef. It came from cattle with BSE or "mad cow disease." Millions of cattle were slaughtered in an attempt to prevent the disease spreading.

◁ **Bird flu can spread to humans.**

In 2005 in Vietnam, a girl died after playing close to chickens that had been infected with bird flu. Other people also became ill and it was clear that the disease had jumped from birds to humans. There is now even more concern because bird flu has spread to other countries, such as Turkey. Here, again, people have died after contact with infected birds.

⬇ **Thousands of people have been poisoned by a germ called E. coli.**

Bacteria like E. coli can pass from raw meat to cooked meat when they are stored close together. This can cause severe food poisoning that can lead to severe illness or even death.

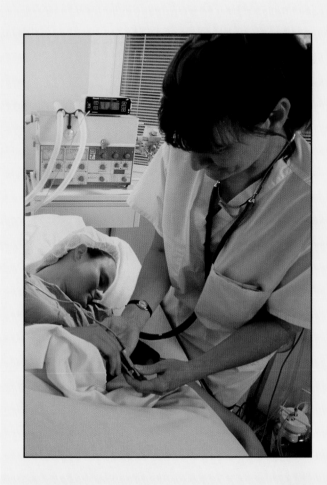

What can you do?

You may live in a country where there is more than enough food to go around.

Visit a farm, and grow something yourself. It will help you learn more about the hard work it takes to produce food.

It is important that you learn about the millions of people who go without adequate food and water. You can also learn about Fair Trade, and what it stands for.

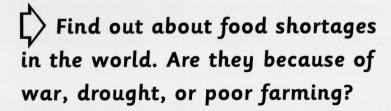 Find out about food shortages in the world. Are they because of war, drought, or poor farming?

Look at these websites:
• Make Trade Fair
www.maketradefair.com
• Friends of the Earth
www.foe.org
• Make Poverty History
www.makepovertyhistory.org
• World Food Day—October 16
www.worldfooddayusa.org

Do a project on your local farm.

Find out what crops are grown and what they are used for. Does the farm grow wheat, barley, or rice? What are these crops used for? Check which of the cattle are for milk and which are for beef. See if the farmer produces vegetables like beets, or fruits like apples. Find out if they are sold in the local market.

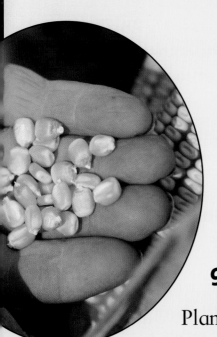

Start a fruit and vegetable garden.

Plant some peas and lettuces and watch how they grow. Even in the classroom you can plant mustard and cress just on moist blotting paper. Remember that not all our food has to come from large-scale farming. You'll understand more about food and farming by having and looking after your own garden.

Glossary

Bacteria—Microscopic organisms with one cell. Some bacteria can cause disease.

Crop rotation—Changing the crops grown on the same piece of land every year.

Fair Trade—An organization that promotes and sells products made by developing countries for a fair price.

GM—Genetically modified. Many plants are genetically modified to stop disease or pests destroying them, or to produce higher yields.

Irrigation—Watering land or crops; pipes or channels are often used.

Malnutrition—An illness or weakness people may have because they do not have enough food to eat or they are not eating enough of the right foods.

Nutritious—Food that is full of the good things our bodies need to stay healthy.

Organic—Growing food or raising animals without using pesticides or chemicals.

Subsistence farming—Growing only enough food to feed your family, with none to sell for profit.

Sustainable farming—Maintaining crops, livestock, and soil by using natural fertilizers and foods.

INDEX

Photocredits

Abbreviations: l-left, r-right, b-bottom, t-top, c-center, m-middle

12–13t – Argentina. Back cover tl, 5tl, 6br, 30br – Brand X Pictures. 1, 10bl, 14–15c, 17br, 20–21tm, 26–27tr, 29br – Corbis. Back cover tr, 3br, 4tr, 7tr, 8–9bm, 11br, 14br, 14–15t, 15br, 16bl, 18br, 18–19t, 19ml, 19br – Corel Stock Photos. 31ml – Comstock. 6–7t – DAJ Digital Images. 13tr, 24bm – Digital Stock. Front cover c, 2mr, 4bl, 9br, 16–17t, 17ml, 21ml, 21br – Digital Vision. 26br, 28c – Ingram Publishing. 28–29b, 28–29t – John Foxx. 8br, 10–11tm, 24–25bm – John Hollingsworth. 3tr, 8–9t, 26–27mr – Ken Hammond/USDA. Front cover tl, tr, 3mr, 5br, 11ml, 20ml, 30–31tm – Photodisc. 23tr, 26bl – Select Pictures. Front cover b, 7bl, 12bl, 13ml, 22mr, 22–23t, 22–23bm, 24–25tm, 27br, – Stockbyte. 25br – Transfair USA.